Broken Glass Amongst the Snow

TCC

BookLeaf Publishing

Presentation by *BookLeaf Publishing*

Web: www.bookleafpub.com

E-mail: info@bookleafpub.com

ISBN: 9789357442046

First edition 2023

DEDICATION

Here's to the past for learning,

the present for living,

and the future as it unfolds.

ACKNOWLEDGEMENT

Thanks to my family, for their stories and for their time.
As the clock ticks on, they share much more than words.

PREFACE

Storytelling has long been a treasure. We find solace in the stories that are shared with us, bring together generations, and last throughout the centuries. Two people meet in a chance happening on a train. Each with different life journeys, but share more than they would know in a glance. Sherry, the woman, wants to reconcile and regather lost coins that her grandfather collected throughout the years. They were stolen by a treacherous band of thieves and sold off to the highest bidders. The man, who will remain unnamed for now, is on a path to regather himself after years of buying and selling patents. Each has vices that serve to divide them from the cyclical state they find themselves in and return them to the grounded, secure state they both crave. The secrets that they carry will find them in the face of death, and decisions will become secrets passing through the snowy mountain hills.

A circle unspoken

His eyes begged to tell secrets that the mouth dare not

It is bright, there is the distant hum of an oncoming train.
Something felt, more than heard.
Two strangers on the same route. Bound to meet by
chance perhaps, yet they each know life to be more.
The train is here now.
This is not a love story, but a poem.

She glared at his silhouette from the platform, spiking a
feeling anew. His form was strong and straight-standing,
though some informality about him seemed skewed.
Perhaps he could create joy in any situation.
Like how not one person casually walks through
a train station. Differing destinations.
Place to place, vacation, work, safe harbor. There is
always somewhere else to be. That is until the day we lay
down and know- that special someone, we are soon to
meet. Some consider it a train, a dear ride. One that none
will truly understand until the conductor's whistle signals
a final close.
Talk she would not, for she too had somewhere to go. A
mission perhaps, and she just found another clue.
A story unfinished. Told to her by her grandfather since
the time he would count her toes.
She discovered in her journeys-
Truth, far more than fiction, is better to sprinkle over
woes.
A story of glory, travel, and shine - all pieced together

with something he called, “once mine.”
She went on her way, with the tarnished addition to the set.
All things lost will be found, unless they are destroyed.

A Window Seat

Faces pressed against the cold glass, a gentle brush of passerby
All they needed to know is, it would be a long ride
That's how trains work. ——
Through the valleys they would sleep, somewhat.
Across ocean tides and vast skies.
It was hard to imagine a more blissful backdrop for such tragedy.
But
it wasn't all bad.

As he waited for the departure, "30 Minutes, Last Call, 30 Minutes," he situated his things in the train car.
He was alone, finally - and he felt a desperate longing, fulfilled. The golf course conversations had drugged him into a deepened
loathing - The conferences had put a shallow grave in his ear. Even his sky-rise apartment, a living space, christened upon stilts felt such a part of the bustling, bustling city that he never felt,
alone. Now,

Finally.
Even here with others,
Serenity flourished, blossoms unveiled

the sweet dew drops would keep this serendipity sustained
as the uprooted begin to heal.

Last Call

As the cold wind blew, she felt it usher her into the
train.
Without it, she would stand in blank thought, whether in
scorching heat or thunderous rain.
Presently, she thought about the walk back on board and
prayed for a pleasant time.
Safe travels and health were near to her heart, as was the
steady
state -
Of finding herself gracious for the things that she had
acquired, keeping her afloat with all that was at stake.

The melody serenaded her onto the train, allowing
herself to stop once inside
She looked around and felt a moment of pride. The last
stop was difficult to process because she was going to a
place she had been before and knew, that the owners
inside were old and near death and reminded her so,
of her grandfather from long ago and thus, she asked
again
he be forgiven for any of his sins.
The thing about money is it passes hands. And
alongside is no shortage of the dreadful plagues of
erroneous kin. She had heard tell of his time in the war,
the coal mine disasters and the bars behind which his
brother had withered away. He felt guilt for destruction
and worried that it would cast him into darkness until
the near end, perhaps beyond. Though the time he spent

with Sherry brought about change and he learned that she, his granddaughter, put into his path a turn. As he told stories and explained the array of coins, she returned a spark to his life, for through her eyes, what she shared was a masterful display of kindness, endeavoring attentiveness and reserve. He stopped speaking of doubt and trifling sorrows, and instead welcomed what was to come-

the weight of the past cast to ashes and not an inkling too soon.

As they sat in the shed on those cold winter nights, they kept each other warm with storytelling delight.

Little did either know that those stories, once alive, would be revived again with each of Sherry's rides.

As she walked now down the aisle, she looked upon the face of her grandfather, her thoughts running wild. He smiled upon her, with her latest find, tested her emotional strength and sent a warmth to replace the mystery that had been running cold. She had left the old man in the shop with flowers for his late wife, held his hand as they cried, reminding each other of past times. The smile she looked upon now, welcomed her back, and she clicked open her suitcase. The mirror inside showed her own face. In her eyes, she saw near replications of his. Sherry looked down at the folder, placing the latest coin inside,

just where her grandfather would have wanted. It was tarnished and worn, but well worth the price. The find of a century, passed through so much strife.

She loved her grandfather and thought heavily now, how dear it must have been to become a warrior and die with a rose-woven crown. Importance Unseen to any but her, she knew that she must carry out what he started and with his death, her own story began to unfold.

Sitting on the train, she asked for a jack and coke, and prayed tell that the soul of her grandfather would find its way to the glory lands, where all good kings roam, Basking in light as the smell drifts in- frankincense and myrrh.

What it is meant to be

From the window, the cold mixed with the warmth of the cabin caused a
Divide between his two selves. The one wanted to go casually meet the woman he had just seen out the window
The other, wanted to get perfectly complacent and sit here in the peace of his surroundings.
He had watched her for a moment as she bent down and picked up something that looked like a coin up from the ground. She took out a small magnifying glass from her pocket
An oddity, which he enjoyed seeing in strangers
Fascinations within life now seemed to be his greatest pleasure after the long days of bore that he found within the same class of brokers he was accustomed to creating potential partnerships with
Inventors came to him to show off their brilliance. Some believed in themselves just enough, but their products were not up to par. Some had not believed in themselves for a long time and finally went out on a whim
Those were the ones that he loved because their ideas were beautifully wild, they just needed someone to tell them.
Which could often be disappointing. Even after hearing it, there was a deep-rooted disbelief.
Which left the giver with no relief. Until the moment of fruition, when finally-
Ideas spring to form bringing with them a conscious commission.

This way

I have said before that this is a poem and I will remind you now.
Hours had passed in quiet solitude.
As he walked out of his cabin, the train rolled.
He was on his way, knowing somehow,
All to do- grab a drink and feel the natural unwinding on the rail was the essence of his destination.
After the brief and fleeting earlier moment, the woman from the window had surpassed his thoughts.
She was a glimpse in the ebbs and flows of life.
Now here she was at the bar. Waiting assuredly for a drink.
She ordered two and for a fleeting moment he thought she had noticed him, but when she turned and walked away without mention,
He stepped forward and saw this scene to another end.
Ordering his drink he looked out the window to a beautiful morning sky.
On his way back, with a clear head, he looked over and saw her
Astonishment, drop dead.
She sat alone.
Two drinks on her tray.
Get an extra for later. A personal way to say
Get there. Get better. And learn to save the day.
For others, for yourself, find
A way.

A story of containment

She had traveled this way for long enough, the thought no longer perturbed
Within walls there is a certain security,
Though for some that pressure seems too much to bear
Which is what he thought he may feel when stepping on the train
This time though with the scenic swallows and the drink of cheer
The confined spaces around him caused no panic or fear
Steadily rocking
To and fro was enough to ease the quiet woes

Babies in cradles or better yet, mothers' arms.
To see now what was once so comforting and warm
The long days of collecting, wadding, listening and debating
Had put them both in a state long past childhood
Here now, a reminder of the sweet life of budding begonias

He wanted dearly to know
Why
Only for a moment though
He was not in the habit of letting lingering thoughts stick around
Opening up his pocket watch, the lid dusted in white,
He pulled out his glass vile, small enough to make

Not a heap but a perfect hill
It was a habit that had not died, as he felt it sustained him
And kept him with a clear mind. This day
He would look around and blow out grief
Then raise the watch up to his face and breathe in
Sweet relief.

Warming

A story of vices, not love
Well in any romantic sense, is
About as lit now as a broken stove
Not wood, where you can find a way,
But gas, and without the connection it
Cannot sustain heat.

A Wave

Delicately walking around at night
Is a matter of respect,
Or perhaps plight
To be the one awake and up, about
Listening to the quiet wistfulness of a sleeping world
Harbored again to the shore
The boat now settles and then the captain must
Be sure to check all the ties, before he can settle
And though he has a trusty crew, there is something about
A leader that must be sure.

There are the waves of sanity that rise and fall
And to know that the motions of the ocean
Are controlled
By a rock in the sky and we believe in love
There is much to be discovered in a world
Where we have made knowledge a cornerstone
To uncover truth and go to places unknown
Biting the bullet of the bitter cold to
See what it is like on top of a mountain untold
Places a flag on the journeys ventured,
Marking the destination as some stay still and bitter
Meeting new people is a lot like that,
So as she sat in her cabin studying,
He walked about.
There would be someone up now-
As he walked though he saw heads down with caps serving as
shelter from restlessness, he had none
There were closed doors and eyes shut
With all the people, how could he be the only waking soul?
Weathering the unrestful truth.

A fascination

Time whittled away as the wooden figures carved
Keepsakes to bring back to those waiting at home
It became as restless as the days at par
When the holes were long and the tempers short
Hit the ball again, and just one more item in the suitcase...
Ideas shot out like carriers from port
With something to lose

Stops were tedious for him as the journey carried on
But for her, they were full of mysteries to be explored
Every coffee shop conversation led her closer to the truth
Stories that were started and stopped too soon

People she met had become pieces of a puzzle
And every synchronicity was like a shovel
Digging deeper into the life she knew
Coins adding up to shed light on a history old and new

What he could not grasp was the fixations of man
When we walk under the stars and see the collections that withstand
The tests of time, wonders amuck
Answering questions that eventually won't mean a fuck

To anyone but those asking and what did he do?
Supply money, support ideas, his solitude askew

In a world like this, he felt alone
Lacking a deeper connection to the whirring drones

Every dream, he possibly stole
Because the idea would die before it could be sold
Now here, he was looking for peace
And while the wheels were moving, his restlessness was finally deceased
Buried in a coffin of uncertainty
So when they stopped, he did what he knew, kicked backed and watched
As the world around him would slowly unfold

He got out today and saw her there
In a small trinket shop where
Oddities were displayed like profound artifacts from an unseen shroud of something yet
Foretold-
She stood there at the glass counter
Haggling it seemed,
She wanted something badly enough
Her face red and her bargain tough
It was clear to him that she knew more about what the owner held in his hand
The passion was radiating from ear to ear
Finally she smiled and transactions passed

And again she walked out and sat on a bench with her looking glass

A coin.
What story could be there?
For the first time he saw money mean something to someone, more deeply than before.

Moving again

Today the rain brought about a cleansing truth
If one could be known, it was showing through
The only thing left to see now was a clouded sky
A mentality of clarity for the once blind

Fresh to start and early to rise,
He decided that he would ask as they ventured this next ride
How to start and what to say
This is what would stain his day

Like coffee on a blank paper
Later to be used for a grocery list
Walking around
He feels stifled in the crowds

The peace that was upon him at the start had begun to fade
Wavering days made him feel like he needed to choose somewhere to be
Something to do
But what he strove for most, he could not soothe
It was a speaker blasting music in a museum for art
Where signs are everywhere to keep quiet

Influenced by the vial, popped open by his thumb
The effects are honest and he approves
They are not to fade too soon, it is just when they do…

He made enough and had built a reserve

Never in his life had money been a source of question.

So the thought of his saving grace being too expensive?
No.
It was a prescription, administered by himself.
He was fast to believe that the best medicines are those dictated by the taker.
Perhaps that is why she ordered two.
Upon circling back to thoughts of her, he got up and casually walked to the dining car.

He saw her at once. What to do was too not within question.
Though alone, he was quite seasoned.
She looked up and saw him standing by her side, also looking up at the daily menu.
When she glanced at him, she immediately felt as if they were meant to be together, in a museum somewhere in New York, looking up at high-end art, preserved through the centuries.

"This is actually a good one," she decided to say.
"Depending of course, on what you like."
He was intrigued by her response to his inquisition, "Is that right?" he said.
Immediately she was struck by his voice. To be sure this is one of those things where she felt like it spoke to her soul and soothed something building inside her.

She softly responded as if whispering to an old friend,
"Word has it, there was once a king who ate it every night for six months."

With that, she stepped forward and ordered a bagel with salmon and cream cheese.
She did not waste her words and spoke fast.
"Also, I want a whiskey, neat, in a chilled glass.
Lemon on the side." and with that she paid.

The next hand

Settle the food, walk towards a dimly lit room.
Deal. The shuffle of the cards was soothing and familiar.
With it came the comfort of something like a phone call from an old friend.
The laughs that reverberate deep.
Deal. The patience of waiting until all of the cards are in front of each player before they are lifted.
The still anticipation creates a circular wall of deafening- silent sound.
Deal. The time finally comes when the hand is lifted and all minds decide
And with that, the cards are played and the dealer awaits.
Until the jeers, cheers, and shuffles start again,
Deal, another hand.

The chill

Snow fell outside
The cool white flakes painted the landscape and created a sense of solemn peace
Mountains stood tall capped with white and a blanket protected all that lie underneath
Snow fell outside

Warm inside
The window seat offered a taste of the chill
A relief

An unplacid pull
The unquiet sense that there was a connection to be made and the source of energy not yet located
With each passing trove of trees, there came a call for action
Snow falling, and heat on the rise

When the chill hits, most settle down
Hibernation, naturally instinctive
While some, they thrive in the winter
Even their outward appearance blends in
And they feel most comforted by howling winds

White snow,
Falling and an unknown resolution
Calling

The fall

The next stop, welcome
As they hustle off the train
The concrete slick from the fallen rain
Like a wristwatch on a deadman, the hour came soon

She was not as ready as she normally was
And this concerned her, as she woke up from a deep slumber
To the train coming to the stop with nine being the number
Unexpected perhaps because it was not on the itinerary

Unusual this was for a train ride, and she had been on many
It was her preferred way to travel because reliability
The promise of no traffic, scheduled stops, and agility
She could count on a steady pace without turbulence
On occasion there was an unpredicted stop
Sometimes for supplies, and emergency, or maintenance
Today she would gather her case, coffee, and patience
The latter may be the hardest to acquire

Perhaps today, she thought she would find an adventure
Usually stops like these had little to explore

And without unique intricacies she usually left deplored
It was snowing outside though, for today, what more could she want

She stepped off the train, gracefully walking with her back straight
As her grandmother always said, practicing will make it natural and alleviate the pain
Most of her habits were built from youth, and curated carefully until they both walked with canes
Owing was not the word she would choose, but through them her life had bloomed

She had almost entered the door when she saw him against a post, wearing-
Black, a color that reveals and deceives,
So much that is not seen
And all of a sudden she felt herself slip

The ice underneath, shifting her to a bow
Time seemed to slow, taking her to the ground
She looked up and he was nowhere around
Then behind her she felt someone grab her arms

Lifting her up, there he was
Looking into her eyes
Nothing spared her from pride's demise
But he cracked a smile and so, did she

There they stood for a moment in shared relief

Walk

One leg in front of the other,
Keep moving on
Easy enough to say to someone with legs instead of stumps
But war takes things of necessity and turns them into commodities
Showing us all how survival mocks us in sheer reverie

Now that, is a darkened view
Shine, shine, see the light through
Some things are just simply put in truth, not pretty but destitute
Until the one who sees it to be true
That the plight is not something that will dampen their flight
That the midnight air will still bring with it refreshing sights
And even some without their eyes, find ways to look past the damned fight

A grandfather old as the hills
Telling stories of liquor stills
Days past and times shared
Funny now, but then brought a scare

In the backwoods of the hot south
The trees shelter from the heat and the drought
One misstep and a life they would lose
To distinguished explosions or the tightening of a noose

But bodies can be made to work
To beautify the land, providing sustenance for the family man
Trained for better and see it through
Day in and day out, we discover what we must do

Today is different

The sun comes up and the clocks tick on
There is a steady rhythm to the turn
Telling the Earth hello again
Scientifically, the pattern is the same,
In reality, many things change

There are people waking up to different songs
And changing their clothes, or their tones
Today was to be no different than that
After all, it was only an unexpected stop
A chance fall and a meeting of two, not to be
separated anytime soon

Telling him about her goal was easy enough
He listened to her at the cafe table.
He had eyes that glistened with wonder, beckoning
for more
So she told him of the stories and her mission, behold
She pulled out folders, her vigor is what sold

Scientifically, magnetism is a natural force
Deciding now was not their choice
He had listened to pitches for some time now
Attention to detail was in his veins
This was different, as she had no aim
No target she seemed to want to hit, only a
conversation she would not tame

In reality, about coins, he had no personal interest-
upon him she betrothed
A fascination with her story, but her passion, like the
sun, shown
And with that, they sat and talked
Unaware of the world around them, people to and fro
Deeply embedded are subconscious truths, that all
will find
When doors close and new possibilities cast
themselves upon a throne

Canard

Commotion greeted them back on the train
Only momentarily and then all was the same
A message over the speaker to return to seats
And so he did after grabbing a bite to eat

It was not that he wasn't hungry at the station
But transfixed in a savvy conversation
What lie ahead though he did not see
For he went back to his cabin, alone to be

To find comfort in the self
Is a measure he meant to take
And though the evenings were long,
Indeed it was a much-needed break

The conversation with Sherry did not deter him
He found it refreshing but ending not a minute too early
Quite fond of her he did leave
But awaiting him in his cabin was a familiar deed

He rested himself upon the cabin couch
Determined to put his mind at ease
He bent into a crouch
From his sock he pulled the vile that for a while seemed to tease

Rarely did he find himself beyond eager for his powder
But something about conversations that lasted over an hour
Brought about a beckoning for him to go
Lose himself again in the inhalant tow

And that he did,
With a flick of his watch
He lifted to his face and hit a notch
Down he felt his trouble sink, and come back soon?
Like a mime refuses to speak- this thought, he would not think

Into the night

Darker and nearer, the night grew
Shelter in the warm hue
The golden fixtures reflected the light
As the train rolled singularly into the night

Not much had been said over the radio
Walking back now from the bar, he stubbed his toe
And what rang out was a silent cry
The feeling of pain rushing blood to the sky

A transfusion of unrequited disbelief
Embarking towards a pleasurable relief
When the feeling passes and normalcy returns
Oh, to be able to heal in such a quick turn

That very wish has been cast into the sea
For things other than minor injuries
Prayers for the big, and the small
Until the lifting of sorrow touches all

Ne'er will come a day, but in it hope can be shared
As such when he saw her there
She had a slight grin upon her face
Though knowing it hurt, he had a collected pace

So she felt it okay to say,
“I was told to watch more carefully in the night than the day,

Just as the horse will stand when it eats
Because if danger comes, it may retreat."

She continued, "Now that toe of yours never saw it coming,
For eyes it has not,
But yours are beautifully placed upon your face
And it seems your attention to obstacles they have wrought."

He replied with a smile,
Adding, "Indeed, your sarcasm falls on listening ears
Though my eyes the subject of occasional breaks, I can assure you, I hear
And from what that chuckle told them so, is that you find amusement in their neglect."

He paused,
Then leaned in and whispered,
"And just to be sure, I'll have you know,
That my sense of feeling works just fine, from head to toe."

His eyes traced her body and returned to meet hers,
Those secrets she now could see came in troves
Part of her wished to become entwined in their coves
Alas, she broke his spell and got up from her seat

With a gentle brush of his shoulder she passed into the aisle
Glancing back and taking note of his candor style
The approach he had was singularly unique

And so it took some effort to shake his air as she went for a drink

Though some may find it cold,
He appreciated her way of without words saying what needed to be told
With her notion, he continued to his cabin
Returning to his business, not a bit saddened

There was humor in this whole bungle
Relief too, both being on the same train
Though they need not stay together, a certain connection remained
Then it came, an almost deafening, and forewarning rain

Bar None

She walked past the darkened reds, greens, and golds
Up to the bar from whence a familiarity had come behold
It was the chosen vice that she felt set her free
Apart from all the other things that cause her tragedy

She had never been one to exceed in much
There was always something that kept her in touch
Reality would have it so that she usually did what she was told
If told of course by her grandfather, up until he was remarkably old

She had been sent on a mission of sort
To pinpoint the lost as a result of such tort
That which beseeched her grandfather, long ago
A thief, credited for the history that he stole

She knew this person could not have acted alone
The whole cast of actors, her grandfather had known
He laid them out for her in clear detail
It was, however, prior to his recovery when they set sail

She was told they not only meant to take what was his in possession
But made claim for his life as their idealized mission
The coins held value, to be sure
The man and his knowledge, however, was the real azure

She flew on the wings of his legacies he shared

Determined to seek justice on those who had dared
Try to stop his heart for their glory
In the days past, how she longed for one more story

She found these vividly in the sets as they resurfaced
The train rides, calls, and antique dealers like serpents
Wriggled around her every move
And became each a masterpiece, as finely curated as such in the Louvre

She wanted a drink now to rinse down an array of emotion
Though, startling so, she found no one to create her potion
A bartender was there around the clock
For there to be none now was a curious shock

She decided to wait, for the result of patience, resolve
But after a while she became concerned and enthralled
Looking behind the curtain, she saw a most disturbing sight
The bar keep, tied to a pole, blood in his teeth

She was familiar with the look in his eyes,
The foreboding nature, pure demise
It reminded her so of the work of the troop
And fear struck her like chickens as a fox approaches the coop
She would not have this happen now
As the latest set was almost complete, but how?
A plan must be created and fast
Her request bespoke the man and untied him at last

She listened to his disoriented rage
(His silence he forlorn swore)
About how a large man, something of a sage

Convinced him to share in drink
What to do now? they must think

She was aware that from here,
A worsening was near
It would only be a matter of time
And now she knew why they stopped at Station Nine

She saw immediately the ploy
A distraction for which she must not toy
Could she trust the man of secrets who caught her?
Or was he too another key destroyer?

She decided to trust herself and take note of what she knew
The people who she had heard tell of were not through
They were still determined to complete their goal
So she would go and see if the man's secrets could be sold

This line is no exception, it is still about her
With all the money in the world, some stories are never told

Don't stop now

What you have not seen are the other passengers on the train,
Each in their own world, with their own pain
Finding that there are, things that help

Greatness is sought after, step by step
Having the will, the determination, the effort to remain
Today, tomorrow, oh- the yesterdays, from the sun back to icy rain

This will take two

His icy blue eyes were now enveloped with red
The numbness in his legs, reminding him of what she said
He felt his toe then, but now, not a chance
The rain had turned to snow and the clock hands danced

He stepped from his cabin to explore
But to his surprise she was walking briskly past his door
When she saw him, her eyes became wet
He looked at her in confusion as she wept and finally asked what it meant

His sincerity rang true through his voice
Reassurance that trusting him was a wise choice
Though she had just recently met this man
She felt that with him, she could take a stand

He listened attentively as she quickly explained
And knew at once that she was not safe on this train
What maniacs unraveled the threads of society
Drove him to curse the insufferable construed propriety

His belief held firm in keeping to oneself unless harm to others was to claim

In all his years he still wrestled with those stricken with a contrary aim
Help her he would, because the mission was clear
That the formerly easy ride of this trip's end be near

A soft landing

The white, uniquely patterned snowflakes stuck to the glass
As a collective, they formed a great, consuming mass
That's the thing with matters that are small,
When enough join together, they become immensely tall

A pinch, a poke, an unwanted stroke
Means nothing at first, until after a while
The toppling pressure of the combined weight-
Is enough to make even the strongest of giants break

So here the two needed each other to hold strong against the avalanche of strife
And though he was high as hell, he pledged that he would fight hand and knife
Up, up, up they ran through each segment of the train.
Nothing seemed out of place, until the blood stain.

They say that blood is thicker than water, but a bride would choose
White wine on her dress above red, and doves are a symbol of peace, not strung up balloons
Each directed towards a certain cause, and necessary to say
But presently on this train, red was a caution to stay away

Carry on, they must because madness was afoot
To blacken the eye and bloody the mouth a barkeep was sign enough
They followed the trail until they reached the final car

The conductor's cabin, where someone sat and had brought them thus far

When they opened the door she knew right away
This was not the same man that was driving the train yesterday
A new person sat, smiling sardonically
He knew her face from anywhere, curses of familiarity

She told the man with her,
Now was the time,
So he put the strap around the false conductor's neck and shouted,
"Grab onto mine!"

Grounding herself,
She grabbed his arm
With his other, watch in hand, he yanked open the door
The face shattered, but rather than the familiar tick, the force of wind and his beating heart roared
Glass scattered and snow blew in
Sherry and the man held tight, mostly unharmed

The dreadful man now limp, they let loose the belt
Then threw him from the opening- a final bitterness had left

The man, now a killer got into the seat where the imposter had sat
And took note of all the commands
Fortunately for all on the train that day,
He was a quick to learn kind of man

When in death's cold embrace,
He remembered what his father said,
"Once you gain something, build on it
And make sure the foundation is solid ground."
Oddly enough today, there was only the cold, biting white snow all around

He drove the train hard through those mountains
Until alas- with great relief, he saw a distant station
Thanks to an old saying- a train is slow to stop,
He braked ahead for the wheels to slow their rotation

When he got up, she saw something glimmer in the seat
A coin remained there, warm from his heat
Handing it to her, proclaiming,
"I believe this is yours."
And together they stepped down from the train's open doors.

If he were to tell his story, it is certain that none would believe
That he drove a train, high on cocaine, through the snow-covered trees
This would be another secret for his eyes to hold,
She would share it with him now, not soon to be told.
This is not a love story,
It is a poem.

www.ingramcontent.com/pod-product-compliance
Lightning Source LLC
Chambersburg PA
CBHW051740130826
49812CB00033B/938
9789357442046